FOREPLAY

Sexual Healing for Spiritual Wholeness

Foreplay
Sexual Healing for Spiritual Wholeness

Jamal-Harrison Bryant

BLOOMING
HOUSE
PUBLISHERS

Unless otherwise indicated, all Scripture quotations are taken from the *King James Version* of the Bible.

FOREPLAY—Sexual Healing for Spiritual Wholeness

Jamal-Harrison Bryant
Empowerment Temple
1505 Eutaw Place
Baltimore, MD 21217

ISBN: 1-892352-63-X
Printed in the United States of America
Copyright © 2004 by Blooming House Publishers

Blooming House Publishers
P.O. Box 11509
Durham, NC 27701

DEDICATION

This book was birthed out of a lot of love.

To my Heavenly Father who sent PERFECT love through his son Jesus.

To my parents who gave UNCONDITIONAL love when I was unbearable.

To my daughter Topaz, who gives PURE love....especially when we're going to Chuck E. Cheese's.

To the members of Empowerment Temple, who express CONSISTENT love as I develop as a pastor and leader.

To Sharon Page and Pamela Crockett for SISTERLY love to see and push the potential of my possibilities, in order to get this book done.

And last but not least.........

To Lady Gizelle, who GOD sent me to show me TRUE love.

To anybody that I forgot to mention I've got nothing but LOVE for ya!

CONTENTS

Introduction

FOREWORD

All too often the questions concerning sexual morality go unanswered and lost amidst the shuffle of church doctrine and legalisms. I'm often flooded with inquiries from the saints seeking guidance and clarity when it comes to putting aside the weights of ungodly, fleshly desires versus disciplining natural affections, and how to distinguish the two. With the institution of marriage under attack, and relationships rapidly taking on a whole new meaning, this is a timely message for the entire body of Christ.

As a young boy growing up, my first sexual experience was during childhood with a woman over 30 years of age. Not realizing the depth of the damage due to this sordid affair, I would go into my adult years wandering about aimlessly from one relationship to the next, trying in vain to fill a void that I had no idea even existed. It wasn't until I accepted Jesus into my life and developed true relation- ship with him that I truly understood the need for healthy intimacy and the proper touch.

Amidst a society of sexually-charged ambience, many struggle with the battles of sensuality and religion, morality and unscrupulous behavior. Jamal Bryant confronts this controversial topic and sheds some much-needed light on the ills that accompany the emotional and mental challenges of the Believer. Answering questions that affect men and women, the reader discovers the unconditional love of God to fill the voids with godly wisdom and sound decision-making. *FOREPLAY— Sexual Healing for Spiritual Wholeness* will help you to realize that sensuality is not an abnormality, but an emotional reaction to a natural attraction. This is your guide to sexual purity!

—Bishop George G. Bloomer
Best-selling Author
When Loving You is Wrong, but I Want to be Right

INTRODUCTION

FOREPLAY—Sexual Healing for Spiritual Wholeness is a testament to my own spiritual development and personal deliverance. One of the invisible enemies to the society of the saved is sexuality. The illicit spirit of fornication runs rampant in many congregations and adultery seems to be the norm around the country. I can attest at 30 years of age, that I've never smoked a cigarette or tasted alcohol. However, the area of my life that had me bound was an affliction of my flesh that led to sordid sexual escapades. I grew up in the church, third generation minister, amidst a nurturing, healthy environment. None of that, however, gave me the discipline to protect my physical temple from ongoing fleshly impulses.

I attended all the church retreats and empowerment conferences, listened to all the tapes, and heard hundreds of sermons. Still, the themes of *Just Say No, Learning to Wait,* and *Abstinence is the Answer,* never seemed to override my will to do the opposite. Just like the prodigal son—who spent all he had on riotous living and women—I didn't come to myself until I woke up in a pig-pen with mud masking my face. Even before the wake-up call, however, the toxicity of my behavior would transcend the borders of my existence and trickle into the lives of those who took pleasure in my deeds. It took becoming a single father, a gold patron for the termination of unwanted pregnancies, almost losing the woman whose love I took for granted, and being an unofficial "travel agent" for imported flights of fancy, before I would even hear the alarm, much less wake up out of the quagmire of confusion of which I'd become entrenched. I was so engrossed in my temporal pleasures that I unknowingly looked like a clown in my efforts to juggle people instead of balls, and transformed into a type of Inspector Gadget in a futile attempt to keep my sins from being discovered, all while professing salvation and servant hood to God and the masses. Albeit a stony journey, I finally concluded that it was indeed time for me to go home to holiness.

It merits mentioning that every woman I was involved with during my riotous escapades was also saved; thereby, revealing that the enslavement to sexuality was a demonic, equal opportunity destroyer. I've come to discern that sinful sexuality amongst the saved is not a habit. Rather, it's a spirit that must be conquered and destroyed! An entire generation could very easily be lost from the kingdom if we continue to put band-aids on areas that require open-heart surgery.

This book is an adaptation from a series that I preached at the most powerful place on the planet—which happens to be the church I'm blessed enough to pastor—Empowerment Temple A.M.E. in Baltimore, Maryland. It was after this series that our ministry began to propel. There was a clear indication that there were many like me who knew they were spiritually out of sync and in need of a relational, psychological and emotional adjustment. It's my prayer that this book helps you begin your journey toward healing and deliverance. For this is simply, *FOREPLAY—Sexual Healing for Spiritual Wholeness*. Penetration won't happen until you make up your mind that you're willing to go all the way with GOD!

—Jamal-Harrison Bryant

Chapter One

LONGING FOR LOVE

More and more, our television and radio waves are being inundated by the overt sexual overtones of a culture that not only expects, but demands the pulchritude of outward perfection. From the advertisement of clothing to the marketing of chewing gum, sensuality has become the motivating factor, bombarding the sensual vulnerability of the American consumer, convincing him to buy...buy...buy. Indeed, it has had a tremendous effect upon our youths who pattern and shape their lives around the core of "what's hot and what's not...who's in and who's out," and love has become something that is barbaric, rather than intimate, spiritual, and sensual. The liberal notion of "anything goes" is no longer the mindset of the minority, but is now the prevailing sentiment of a generation whose ideologies possess the power to shape the posterity of those to come.

The hours of crude videos and ignorant comedians who impose their liberal views of misguidance upon our youthful generation have sent a poor signal to misguided young men who feel that the depth of touching a woman's sensuality is covered in platinum or a Bentley with chrome rims. The television screen is inundated with women in bikinis sitting on the hoods of high-priced cars as men bellow in the background with no intonation

13

toward intimacy. It's an alien encounter by which neither party ever gets to know the other, much less develop a healthy relationship under the banner of a Christian-guided relationship.

We've all heard the countless, controversial, in-your-face lyrics, which present a blueprint of conjured-up romanticism with no foundation from which to stand. None of these songs deal with romancing the mind, becoming one in spirit and embracing the totality of another's very being. So I would dare say that we can not, then, simply blame America or one specific culture in society, but rather, the blame lies upon what we have done to ourselves. Matthew 24:12 says, *And because iniquity shall abound, the love of many shall wax cold.* We have made it common fare to call the women, whom we profess to love, female dogs and farming equipment, with no accountability or responsibility for nurturing them in the bare essence of their soul and womanhood. It is a foreign asterisk, lost in the annals of time, to find on television a man opening the door for a woman, or to witness a brother treating a sister with dignity and respect. In fact, now that we have found ourselves in a hip-hop, gangster-rap, and hard-rock mentality, we see behavior that is barbaric in areas where we ought to operate out of intimacy. Many of us have not been able to decipher and discern the distinction between an intimate relationship versus an alien relationship.

INTIMACY VERSUS EROTICISM

An intimate relationship can be defined as closeness within the privacy of personal space. Conversely, an alien relationship is simply an impersonal experience. You roll out of bed and don't even recognize the person lying next to you, don't know the individual's first or last name, or that person's origin. It's a destructive lifestyle of being led by eroticism, rather than the gift of intimacy, closeness, and effective communication with the one who has been assigned to your destiny. Though many profess to be Christians, they base their realities and relationships on a lost-ark mentality, unknowingly becoming seekers and destroyers of flesh instead of instruments of life. Intoxicated in your own lust, you can easily become oblivious to the fact that God has called you to have a healthy and intimate relationship. You can not have an intimate relationship with someone you do not know. The most precious and private thing that you possess is your sexuality. Giving your sexuality away sends a signal that you no longer respect or value your most prized possession—yourself.

While visiting Atlanta some time ago, I went into a shoe store to purchase a pair of shoes that were displayed in the window. I went upstairs and asked the sales clerk for the shoes in a size twelve so that I could try them on. Much to my disappointment, however, when He brought the pair of shoes out, I did not recognize them.

"No, I want the pair of shoes that are in the window," I kindly reminded him.

He responded, "Sir, these are the exact same pair of shoes."

I disagreed, "These can't possibly be the same kind of shoes, because they don't have the same color; they don't have the same fit, and they are not the same shape."

He explained, "Sir, the problem is that although they are the exact same pair of shoes, many people have tried this pair on, and the constant trying on of the shoes has caused them to lose their color, as well as their shape, and form."

Subsequently, I began to receive a revelation as I thought, "The same thing is going to happen when God comes back for His children. He is going to say, 'You are not the person that I ordained you to be, and you don't look like the person that I created because you've allowed too many people to try you on. Therefore, you've lost your color; you've lost your shape, and you've lost your form."

Though many of us are more apt to deal with sexuality while ignoring sensuality, we can not discuss one without confronting the other. Your sexuality is based upon and immersed in your sensuality. Your sexuality is activation, while your sensuality is motivation. You become a sexual creature before you ever commit the actual act of physical intimacy. Simply put, this means that your sexuality is not based upon your sexual organs, but instead your sensual glands. You have five areas of sensuality. So, what are you allowing yourself to see, hear, touch, feel, and taste? What you allow yourself to sense the most will prompt or motivate you sexually.

THE POWERFUL VOICE OF THOUGHT

You commit sin, not just by actions, but also by your thoughts. You may have already committed a sin and experienced multiple orgasms of adultery and fornication sitting right in church, with an innocent party, whom you've never met, and whose name you don't even know! Proverbs 23:7 reminds us, ...*as he thinketh in his heart, so is he.* Lack of physical contact does not make one guiltless of sin.

You are sensual before you are sexual because your sexual drive is first prompted by what you see and/or hear. Once it's seen, your mind decides, "I want it." If you then proceed to touch it, you've moved even further into the danger zone because now you're convinced, "I have to have it!" But more than that, if you can touch it and see it, it occupies your space. This is a realm of sensuality that you may not be able to handle because it will inevitably lead you to sexuality. There is a certain part of each of us, which is vulnerable to the touch—one of the many vehicles, which can usher us into sexuality and keep us trapped in our own sexual delusions long after the experience has occurred. The actual act of sexual contact repeatedly playing the experience in your mind becomes the driving force behind your anticipation for future and ongoing encounters.

For some who are saved and have been removed from sexual activity for a long time, it is easier to stay saved, because the memory of the experience is not as fresh as those who actually indulge in ongoing sexual desires. Then there are those who must seclude themselves in order to resist its magnetizing temptation. ⸥ The closer you are to the grasp of temptation, the tougher it is to remain free. The first few days of the initial temptation are usually the most gruesome, as your mind and emotions race around a cesspool of confusion and seemingly unbearable enticement. You begin making cameo appearances in the editor's cut of your own conjured-up movie thrillers of passion and deceit. Songs of days gone by trigger untapped emotions, so you begin to warn those around you, "I need space and time to gather myself," because you understand the importance of protecting your sexuality. You count the daily battles as victories inching you closer and closer toward winning the ultimate war. That is why it is so important to seek godly counsel before entering marriage and lifelong commitments. Being paired with the right person lessons the risk of seeking fulfillment in other domains.

SEEKING MR. RIGHT

I often warn women who are contemplating marriage to marry someone who can take care of them. When a woman marries, it ought to be to someone who is capable of taking her to the next level. If she comes from poverty, there is no reason for her to get married and still be impoverished. The role of the man is to take her to another place. When she gets married, she ought to dress better, drive better, live better, and eat better, not constantly be in a struggle over where her next meal is coming from. My grandmother used to say, "I can do bad all by myself!"

For women desiring a mate, the objective, of course, would be to find a Christian man, who's settled, has goals, accomplishments and a job. But a goal-oriented and focused man can't just be approached any kind of way. So the woman who seeks this type of stability must make sure that she stands out above the crowd:

1. Make sure your relationship with the Lord is strong and growing.
2. Make sure that you are presentable. Working from the inside out, your presentation should be representative of both who you are and whom you seek. Appearance is a reflection of how you see yourself.
3. Have the ability to hold an intelligent conversation.
4. And most importantly, allow the Holy Spirit to take control. You don't need to go after him. He's going to come after you, because after he sees and smells you and knows that you're in his presence, he's going to want to know who you are! I know there's somebody reading this book who has been chasing after the "man of your dreams," but God says, "Just sit still and allow patience to have her perfect work through Me."

Furthermore, it's never a good idea to be too forward and too aggressive. Attempting to win a man's affections by jumping into bed with him will only backfire and cause him to lose interest in ever developing a lasting relationship. It causes him to lose respect for you and question your character. However, if he sees that you are dressed with quality, that you smell like you are somebody, that you look like you're doing fine without him, then that will attract the right attention from him. He'll have no choice but to give you his attention. Stop looking so needy, climbing into bed, trying in vain to capture a man's heart.

God woke me up in the middle of the night and said, "The same thing that Naomi told Ruth to do is the same thing that I want them to do for me." God is so sick of saints coming to Him trying to get a quickie and never romancing Him for Who he is—going to church screaming, shouting and hollering, but hadn't been intimate with God all week long! Stop trying to treat God like a sugar daddy and start romancing Him with worship and praise: "I'm yours Lord...everything I've got...everything I'm not!"

The God we serve, which is the God of love, demands and requires of us foreplay before He gives us what we need. In the book of Ruth, the mother-in law tells Ruth, "You have to wash." John 15:3 reminds us, *Now ye are **clean** through the word which I have spoken unto you.* When you sit in the Gospel of Jesus Christ, you are taking a shower. When you hear the unadulterated Word of God, then the dirt and grime that you've accumulated all week long begins to wash off of you. Ask God to "create in you a clean heart and renew a right spirit." Stand in the word. Then wait upon the Lord to renew your strength.

Naomi told Ruth to put on expensive perfume because she understood the correlation between sensuality and sexuality. She said, in essence, that if you motivate his sense of smell, then it will activate his response. You may be saying to yourself, "I don't understand where I can get a perfume that will get God's attention." No, I'm not talking about Issey Miyake. This is not a job for Jivago or Gucci Rush. But if we're to mirror the image and life of our Father, we must *walk in love, as Christ also hath loved us, and hath given himself for us an offering and a sacrifice to God for a sweetsmelling savour.* You get God's attention by putting on the "aroma of Christ." I know that we've been taught to believe that we ought to walk like Jesus. We ought to talk like Jesus. We ought to live like Jesus. But rarely were we told that we need to smell like Jesus. You smell like Jesus when you have the anointing.

This "sweetsmelling savour" gives two different and distinct aromas and has a dual function:
1. It repels the enemy. Some folks can sniff out that you're saved, which is why they ponder their approach before approaching you. They realize that there is something unique about you that won't allow you to tolerate foolishness.
2. It brings a blessing to you because the angels descend when they smell you, because they know

that Jesus is close by. Some have been known to have the opposite affect—repel, instead of attract—because they put on too much of the wrong things. There is something about being sprayed with the anointing of God that arrests the hands of the enemy and prevents the traumas of life from driving you crazy. Instead of staying up all night tossing and turning, you find yourself asleep with the peace of God that surpasses all human understanding. Sometimes you have to understand what anointed perfume does. I found out that some prayers will not change people. No matter how long you pray for them, they are going to remain the same. They were born mean, they're living mean, and they're going to die mean. I've found that no matter how much you pray, sometimes God won't change situations. Consequently, sometimes prayer may not change people or their situations, but it will change how they look at people and how they look at their situations! From this day forth, stop giving people too much power and authority over your life.

3. Another thing that Naomi tells Ruth is, "Put on your best outfit." God said, "If you really want to turn me on, if you really want to get my attention, dress up in what I bought you—the whole armor of God. Put on the breastplate of righteousness, the shield of faith, and the sword of the spirit."

THE REWARDS OF LASTING COMMITMENTS

In Ruth, Boaz said, "I appreciate you because you waited on me." God is saying, you had other opportunities to be with someone who is not saved, but because you walked away from the carnality of temporal satisfaction and decided, "I'd rather be faithful and wait on the God of my salvation," He's vowed to now make you ruler over many."

Boaz told Ruth (Ruth 3:15), "Bring me your vail." He put barley in the vail because he understood as a good provider that he had to give her resources after he slept with her. One night stands leave you empty and wanting with an inexplicable void that can not be filled. But God said, "If you just sit at my feet, I'm going to give you so much that you will not have room enough to receive—pressed down, shaken together, and running over."

Perhaps you're trying to figure out why you are driving what you drive, how you're eating what you eat, or living where you live, but it's all because you woke up. Even when you thought about sleeping in the bed, and when you forgot to turn your clock forward, God said, "Because you rush to get to church on Sunday mornings, I'm going to bless you with the desires of your heart."

Perhaps your reputation seems to have suffered irreparable damage from sleeping around, but when you sleep with God, He restores bad reputations and He is One who won't let you go until He blesses you. When you look back over your life, and you think about what God has done for you and see how He's elevated you and see how He's made a way for you, I'm sure you can testify to the fact that there is no better partner than the partnership with God.

What you need from God may not manifest today, but if you keep praying, meditating on His Word and worshipping Him, before you know it, everything that you've been needing God to do will manifest. God has something wonderful for you, if you just learn to turn Him on and tune needless distractions out! If you want to get God's attention, praise God like you need Him. There is a prerequisite to being blessed. You can't just jump in the church asking God to do stuff for you when you haven't done anything for Him. God said this is a two-way operation. If you need God to turn you out, you must turn him on, and learn how to fight to keep what rightfully belongs to you according to the Word of God! Let's now find out how to maintain this relationship of true intimacy through knowledge, insight, and safeguarding the love of God and His Word, which is hidden in your heart.

Chapter Two

HANDLING HANNIBAL

There is an unseen enemy who desires to sift you as wheat, have his one night stand of temporal pleasure and leave you destroyed for a lifetime. Hosea 4:6 says, "My people are destroyed for lack of knowledge." Time and time again we see the truth of this Word revealed and proven through ignorance, *mis-education*, and gross injustices. And because the roots of ignorance often run so deep, few even notice that they've even been robbed or cheated of information beneficial to the betterment of their existence, stimulation of mind, and growth. The most prevalent example of ignorance and lack of knowledge is when we deal with entertainment, confusing and convoluting it with education.

HANDLING HANNIBAL

For instance, Hannibal, as we first knew the name, was a defender of the Carthaginian people. After rising to power in 221 BC, he was able to wage war and fight off the entire Roman Empire. He was a fighter and a defender. Within recent vintage, however, because of the mis-education of America, they've transformed Hannibal from a defender into a devourer, and given him the name, Hannibal Lector. Consequently, children who have not been properly educated, and hear the name Hannibal, automatically associate that name with someone who is a devourer, rather than the great defender that his name originally bore witness of throughout history.

We find ourselves caught in warped sociological synonyms where things have the same name, but possess different meanings. Although God created man as a defender, many women who hear the Word "man," often equate him with a devourer, when that name is supposed to provoke feelings of security and comfort. When women hear the word "man," they will, in fact, give a universal umbrella that all men are dogs. Their limited experiences show all men as devourers and not defenders.

How then do we so morbidly misconstrue what God has created. God has created the man to be a defender, but through the lens of misrepresentation, he is transformed into a devourer. Likewise, when you deal with the word *Christian,* you will also often find some warped meaning—a duality of purpose. There are some Christians who are defenders of the faith, but then there are others who are devourers of the faith. These Christians don't stand up for God, but fall for anything that comes their way. Unsaved loved ones of Christians often can not determine what to call those who profess Christianity because the Christian is often undecided as to what to call himself.

DEFENDERS OF FAITH

When you cannot defend who you are—a defender or a devourer—you find yourself in the vice grip of the devil's claws. The devil wants to transform you from your original purpose, which is to defend life, and instead, take you into a lower stratum where you are the taker of life.

Your actions speak louder than the words you profess out of your mouth. *Keep thy heart with all diligence; for out of it are the issues of life* (Proverbs 4:23). Regardless of your confession, your action are ultimately the voice that characterize who you are, your likes and dislikes, your goals and ambitions. For instance, if you tell God that you want long life, but continually abuse your body with the toxins of cigarette smoke and alcohol, what message are you really sending? If there is a generational curse of alcoholism in your family, why then are you further opening the door to the devil under the auspicious title of being a "casual drinker." Your actions determine whether you're a defender or a devourer. Are you something that protects life or something that snatches life?

Many are tossed between two opinions. They don't know whether to give life or take life, though they have no power to give or take. All they can do is preserve life, because God is the giver and taker of all life. So what right does anyone have to tell you who you are going to be, when God created you to speak life into your own situation?

For a fresh prospective on your lifestyle, consider the 21st Century depiction of Hannibal and you will agree that there is something strange in the cinematic presentation of Hannibal. We find somebody twisted and deranged, yet very intelligent. The female protagonist is an attorney by the name of Clarise. She finds herself traveling across the country, all the way to Italy, looking for somebody who tried to take her life. When God gives you a way out of a bad situation, don't crawl back. Walk out and don't look back! What God dropped in my spirit is that sometimes we chase after that which God has delivered us from. God releases a certain person from your life and frees you from a bad situation, but you find yourself dialing that individual's number, and making excuses for the call, "I'm just calling to see how they're doing." Hang the phone up!

DIABOLICAL CONSPIRACY

When you realize that there is a diabolical and demonic scheme to revoke your sanity and devour your life, you can then discern the imps, which have been assigned to you by name. There are some people that the devil keeps flaunting in your path and whenever you feel good, they try to make you feel bad. Have you ever found that there is a family member, whom, every time you get a raise, every time you get a promotion, every time you get your life back on track, attempts to tear down with negative innuendos, everything that you've built. They make statements like, "You ain't all that!" or "I knew you when...!" Just bless them by saying, "What God did for me, he'll double it for you!"

Your enemies come after you to devour your flesh. Understand that not only is satan smart, he is also insightful. You might as well put on your life jacket and brace yourself for the tumultuous waves because he knows that once you got saved, you bought an insurance policy, which means that nobody can touch your soul. And because he can't touch your soul, he'll go after you body. The devil tries to get through your body to contaminate your soul and infiltrate your mind. So the greatest threat against you is your flesh. The devil understands that the more your anointing increases, the more your sexual drive increases.

Before David became anointed, he was in the backyard mowing the lawn. But when God anointed him to be king, he probably found himself tempted on numerous occasions with sexual affairs. The problem with the church is that it tries to neuter you to become asexual—to act like you don't have the drive, the proclivities, and the feelings that you feel, as if you are from some monastery, void of sensuality, incapable of being affected by temptations and sexual feelings.

The Bible says that satan came after Job's flesh. You have to understand that the devil comes after your flesh because if he gets to your flesh, then he can mess with your spirit. When the devil gets a hold of your body, he has a leasing agreement with your mind! In other words, there are some people reading this book, whose body is in one location, but whose mind is on the other side of town! They can't think about what God has done for their spirit because they're distracted by the memories of what has happened to their flesh.

Job lost all of his material gain. His material possessions were an expression of him. In fact, when he lost his possessions, he said, "The Lord giveth and the Lord taketh away." But when the Lord allowed the devil to touch his body, when he shaved his head, sat on an ash heap and began to curse the day he was born, it was at that point that his body got touched. His wife showed up with even more discouragement, "Why don't you curse God and die!"

Let's consider a more practical analysis. If you sleep with somebody and wake up the next morning and find that the person has left and stolen money from your purse, you will more than likely chalk it up as a loss and call that person a thief. But if you sleep with a person and afterwards don't hear from that individual for two weeks, then they didn't steal some "thing" from you, they stole you! And because they stole you, and because intimacy is part of your spiritual nature, you begin to actualize that you don't want yourself to be stolen.

The problem with some of us is that after we are saved, we try to reconcile that we are no longer sexual. That's a lie! You must come to terms with your sexuality in terms of your spirituality. Perhaps you've been conditioned that whatever you feel in your internal nature, is equated to sexuality when oft times its spirituality. So you call Jesus your husband because you have supernatural orgasms thinking that the move of the spirit is something sexual when we have not equated it to something spiritual. I think I better go to a little bit further. Some congregants are attracted to their pastor, and don't even know why. In actuality, it is not the pastor himself, but it's the spirit that is in the pastor that provokes the magnetizing attraction. It is hard to be saved and asexual when you have never been challenged to redirect your sexual energy into spiritual energy. God has to transform your thinking to understand that your body is not your own. Your body is a living sanctuary, pure and holy, tried and true.

MUZZLING THE MOUTH OF TEMPTATION

Learn to put your sexuality under the submission of your spirituality. In the movie, *The Silence of the Lambs*, once they captured Hannibal, the first thing they had to do is muzzle his mouth, because the devil will talk you into anything. There's normally at least one person in your life, whom you're vulnerable to or have been vulnerable to, who has been strategically placed in your life to keep your focus veered off course. No matter what time that individual calls, day or night, you'll leave your job in the middle of the day, or leave chicken baking in the oven at dinner time in order to meet the demands and desires of your inescapable distraction.

There's something about hearing him or her speak that causes you to throw caution to the wind and yield to the voice of temptation time and time again. But when you learn how to shut the devil's mouth and announce, "If God be for me, what in the world can be against me!" then, you're well on your way to eliminating the devourer from your life and walking in great victory. John 8:36 reminds us, *If the Son therefore shall make you free, ye shall be free indeed.* So when the phone rings, make good use of God's gift of caller ID. When the tempter calls, don't even answer the phone. When he comes knocking on the door, remind yourself of the trap that lies on the other side, and deny him entry into your newfound freedom.

In the movie, not only do they put a muzzle on his mouth, but after they captured Hannibal, the second thing they did was handcuff his hands. They had to handcuff his hands because they knew if Hannibal ever put his hands on them that they wouldn't survive. There is something metaphysical to the spiritual being that desires to be touched. That's why the old church used to sing, "He Touched Me!" But because so many people touch you during the course of the week, when you do finally feel the hand of God, you don't recognize it because there have been so many hands touching you already. That is why I don't allow everybody to lay hands on me.

You must disarm your adversary by placing an unreachable gap between yourself and those who are meaning to do you evil. The reality is, because God has given you a poised sense of discernment, you know people who are after you just for your body, and are not interested in your mind and can not help cultivate your spirit. You must possess a you-can't-touch-this mentality to guard yourself from the devourer's touch. Know that when God touches you, then you won't need flesh to hold your hand. You won't need a holy hug. You won't need the target of your vulnerability tapping on the door to *see if you're all right*, because you've been touched by the hand of God, and that becomes your testimony.

Remember, *the weapons of your warfare are not carnal, but mighty through God to the pulling down of strong holds* (2 Cor. 10:4). Though your weakness is presented in the form of flesh, the true target is an unseen enemy—a spiritual demonic stronghold that desires to tear down your commitment and honor to God. To effectively annihilate him, you must...

1. Muzzle the mouth of the enemy with the Word of God. When Jesus was on the mount of Olives, satan came presenting temptation. Of course, Jesus muzzles the mouth of the devil—not by engaging in a physical brawl—but with the indisputable Word of God.
2. Then you must handcuff him. *When the enemy shall come in like a flood, the Spirit of the LORD shall lift up a standard against him* (Isa. 59:19). You may be reading this book and find what Shakespeare has deemed a reversal of

fortune. You have the reversal of fortune because you sit in the sanctuary with a sex partner. Because you sit in the sanctuary with this sex partner, the devil has placed a muzzle on your mouth, and he's handcuffed your hands, because of the guilt and sting of sin that lurks near. You will never be able to muzzle or handcuff the nemesis of your own life if you have become the one devouring the life of another. Church is not supposed to be a social club of gathering to collect phone numbers, but a spiritual institution of healing and restoration. Allow the Lord to transform you and turn your life around.

3. Now that the enemy has been bound and chained, remember that his ultimate goal is still to coerce you to free him again. The book of Psalms says, *For in the time of trouble, he shall hide me...*(Ps. 27:5). That means that whenever you find yourself lighting up incense, playing soft music, and dimming the lights, those are the times that you can't afford to wait until Sunday morning, but you must learn how to praise God in your living room and He will turn your situation around. When you praise Him in the midst of your message, God will leave you with an undeniable message of His omnipotent power.

Oft times in church, we pray for the "exaggerated sin," but dismiss the subtleties of sin. So we, in fact, pray for deliverance for the homosexual and never say anything about the repeat offender fornicator. We'll deal with the men's issues but not deal with the spirit of lesbianism. There are church folks who are bisexual. There are many Christians who don't have a problem drinking, don't have a problem smoking, don't gamble, but still wrestle with one issue of covert sin. Right now, if you're suffering from secret sins, you can't even begin to imagine God blowing your mind by speaking life to your dead situation. Regardless of your struggles, don't ever turn yourself over to your sins. Continue to earnestly fight and God will deliver you and give you an entire lifestyle makeover. When the devil gets into your body, he infuses your spirit. You keep trying to figure out why you draw and attract the same type of people. It's not because of what you're wearing, but because your spirit has sent out a signal that announces, "This is what I'm all about!"

Though you want to do good, you continually find yourself face to face with your undeniable temptations. Paul said, ...*when I would do good, evil is present with me...* (Romans 7:21). You absolutely love God, know all the songs, but it's that one area of your life that you're trying to get through. In Second Corinthians 12:9, however, the Word of the Lord issues a gratifying ray of hope: *My grace is sufficient for thee: for my strength is made perfect in weakness.* Love shouldn't hurt and pleasure should not invoke pain. You must kill the desires of your flesh before your desires kill you!

Chapter Three

LOVE ISN'T SUPPOSED TO HURT LIKE THIS!

I am intrigued to know whether it be through Congress or the Constitution, how many lives have to be stolen before it's appropriate to declare war. All of us are aware of the terrorist acts of a nation under attack, but few of us are aware of the fact that many of our women are under terrorist attack daily. At what point will the president hold a press conference to derive at a strategy by which we can duly and swiftly bring end the terrorization of women, which is taking place everyday within our nation.

Little is often said about the abuse that is silently taking place in the suburbs of Baltimore and the inner cities throughout this nation. If the government is not apprised of the startling statistics, then they need know that ninety-two percent of all violent incidents are perpetrated by men, against women. Three fourths of women who report being raped or abused violently, say that their perpetrators are somebody with whom they are intimately involved. Ten thousand women a year are killed due to domestic violence by somebody they are married to, estranged, divorced or separated from. Forty percent of teenage girls between the ages of fourteen and seventeen, can testify that they know someone personally who is abused. Whether they are slapped, punched or verbally abused, they are suffering abuse by someone with whom they are involved or entranced. Thirteen thousand acts of violence occur on any given work day against women by their estranged intimates. Eighty-four percent of those who come into the emergency room between 11 p.m. and 4 a.m., are women who are there under the guise of an emergency crisis by someone who holds a key to their home. If you don't feel that this is an emergency situation, then obviously you have slipped into a coma and are daydreaming in your personalized Neverland.

The longer we leave our women unprotected and uncovered, the longer it will take for our children to reach emotional and mental wholeness. Most children—eighty-two percent, according to a poll— who have witnessed and lived through abuse of any kind grow up to become adult perpetrators of the violence they've witnessed themselves. The church has remained silent for too long, while being aware of the violence that is taking place in the home of their constituents and their congregants. While women continue to come to church with sunglasses and extra coats of makeup to cover up that which they have endured throughout the week, we don't remind them that Jesus was wounded for our transgressions. He was bruised for our iniquities; so no one has the right to bruise them physically or emotionally, because by his stripes we are healed.

At some point, as the body of Christ, we have to round up and rally and declare war on any acts of violence that are afflicted against our women and our children. To do anything less than that is counter to the cause and the will of our Savior Jesus Christ. So I speak today without any backing of the Pentagon or other governing powers, but by the power of the Holy Ghost, declaring that the blood of Jesus will rest on every woman within our communities who has been abused at the hands of some man, even when the church does not address or eradicate the problem. In the same wise, I'd like to address each man who's reading this book by declaring, "The last time you abused the woman in your life, was indeed the *last* time." We are now raising a generation of men who will not only be responsible, but be accountable for the protection and preservation of our women and children.

TROUBLES OF TAMAR

If war is going to be declared abroad, then we must also declare war on the enemy front that is hitting us at home. This is nothing new, but it's as old as the Bible. We find a crystal clear example in the second book of Samuel. Absalom, the son of David, had a lovely sister, named Tamar. Amnon, also the son of David loved her. This is the origin of the problem—Amnon is in love with his sister. So we're not just dealing with abuse, but we're dealing with incest. Incest is a silent killer that is destroying not only our women, but our children.

The problem is further exaggerated when we find that Amnon is twenty-two years of age and his sister Tamar is only fifteen. We have a similar problem today. Right under our noses thirteen-year-old mothers are walking the hallways of our schools, pregnant by men who are twenty fiver years of age and older. These young girls are not even comfortable with their puberty yet, much less the responsibilities that accompany motherhood. The adult men who impregnate them can't handle the responsibility that entails being with a real woman, so they seduce children in order to have their way. Shame on you parents who are allowing grown men in your homes to date your under-age daughters. Many parents are guilty culprits because they allow themselves to be beguiled by gifts...a VCR for the family, a new refrigerator, or financial assistance when the rent is past due. Later for him! Let him take care of his own mother and you raise your child. No amount of gifts are worth the emotional and psychological setbacks of a child who is attempting to satisfy the perverse passions of an adult. The even less addressed problem is that quite often the teenage mother is a victim of rape or incest. Have you ever looked at a pregnant teenager and thought, "This child is bringing a baby into the world because some man she probably trusted has violated her."

There is a problem in the second book of Samuel because an older man is seducing and is infatuated with a child. But it gets even worse. Amnon was so distressed over his sister Tamar that he became sick. He became sick, not just physically, but also mentally and emotionally. Women, don't think it's flattering or normal for a man to become incapacitated because he is in love with you. If it is a genuine, divine love, then it ought not make him sick. It ought to make him healthy. As a woman, you are a life-giver and not a life-taker. So if he is sick all the time, that ought to be the signal that you're in the wrong place at the wrong time.

He's sick in his mind. Any man who has sexual fantasies about a child or an adolescent is nothing more than sick because he's lusting after a child. No, he has not been contaminated by some music video that he saw on television, but something is wrong with his mind. Don't make the drastic mistake of thinking that you're just going to love him to wholeness. Rather, psychological evaluation and a touch from the Lord is the wholeness that he truly needs.

In Samuel, you'll find that Amnon had a friend whose name was Jonadab, the son of Shimeah, the son of David's brother. Now Jonadab was a very crafty man. He is, in fact, Amnon's friend. Jonadab, at thirty-five is giving advice to Amnon. The object of attention within this circle is a fifteen-year-old girl who's being lusted after by a twenty-two-year-old man, who is receiving advice on the street from a thirty-five-year-old man. The problem with so many of our young boys is that they have been corrupted in their thinking by deranged *older* men, who tell them that their manhood is based on how many children they produce and how many women they have calling their pager. That does not make a man. What makes you a man is going to church, lifting up holy hands and earnestly confessing to God your weaknesses and vulnerabilities while submitting to His will.

Amnon was messed up because he listened to the wrong man for advice. Men should exercise the utmost caution regarding their source of relationship advice, because sometimes your brother will get you in more trouble listening to him than what you were in before you started. Every man ought to find another saved man to be his counsel, his conscience, and his guidance—

one who's not afraid to say, "Brother, you're wrong, and you're about to destroy your entire life and the lives of those who love you." If you can't control yourself, you must continually pray to God, "God take everything away from me that is not like you." I'm tired of men who can't share what they're going through because they're so insecure that they think it will make them look weak or make them look like less than a man. What makes you more of a man is when you understand, "I don't know all the answers, but I do know a God who walks with me and talks with me."

This older man Jonadab, then gives Amnon ungodly advice and counsel:

"This is what you should do. Act like you're sick and get Tamar to bring you something to make you feel better. And when she gets there, seduce her and have your way with her."

A lot of men, with ill intentions will seduce women. They will help women, not because they have a heart for them, but because they have another agenda. And after they've accomplished their agenda, they don't want anything else to do with her. Have you ever been there? When you first started dating, before you gave in to him sexually, he was taking you to dinner, shopping, and the trips never ceased. But now that you've given, the gifts suddenly cease and you wait by the phone for a call that never comes.

Tamar, being a good sister, went to her brother Amnon's house to make him something to eat—trying to take care of a brother when he's down. Once she arrives, he asks everyone else to leave the room. He then tells Tamar, "I'm not really sick. I'm not really hungry. I'm only wanting of one thing, and that is to have you—if only for one night!" And Tamar who is a saved woman says, "Brother, please, don't even trip. You must not know who I am." She says, "If you want to sleep with me, then go see the king. And the king will then release you, but you have to marry me first." Ladies, make sure that any brother you want to be involved with knows how to talk to God. If he doesn't know how to talk to God, then he's the wrong one. Tell him to take the designer shoes and handbags, take the cubic zirconium earrings and leave you with Jesus. You will be all right.

Tamar continued pleading, "Brother, please don't do this. We're from Israel and we don't act this way." Israel is the place of God's chosen people. There's something that ought to differentiate people who are in the church from those of the world. And the reason that I'm addressing this subject is because the abuse that's being inflicted is not just by people who are unsaved, but also being perpetrated by people who are saved. If you are reading this book while lying in bed next to an abuser, or if you're on the way home to the callous welcome of your perpetrator, you *can* be loosed today and set free!

ASSAULTED BY ROYALTY

Tamar tried in vain to reason with him: "Don't do this! You don't understand who you are...you're a child of the king!" Amnon was the crown prince, which meant that he was eldest son. He had wealth. He had influence. And he had power. Still, the only thing that mattered to him at that moment was quenching his perverse passions through the woman he'd been fantasizing about for so long—his sister. So she reminded him, "You're going to blow everything because you're not being responsible for who you are." Many men, in the moments of rage and unbridled lust, lose perspective of who they are and what they are called to be. There is more to you than just another sexual conquest and a notch on your belt. You have to come to your senses and remember, *God did not save me just for this. He didn't save me so that I could abuse women, but he saved me to protect them.* At some point, you must take responsibility for your own actions, realize that you're not only damaging your life, but destroying the lives of others as well, and make a conscious decision to make a life-altering change for the better.

Tamar asks, "After you do this, where will I go? What will I do? You will make me lose all honor and integrity. But not only that, *you* will look like a fool." The bible shares with us, that he still did not listen to his sister, but he forced her to sleep with him and then he left her. I'm talking and ministering to every woman reading this book…It is not your fault that you were abused, and no longer do you have to gravitate toward abusiveness, but now is the time to realize that you too are royalty and deserve God's best. If he hit you once, that was one time too many. He'll give you all good reasons for this *mistake*: "I didn't mean it…I love you…I promise it will never happen again…." Regardless of who he is or the promises that he makes, you must walk through his smoke screen of lies and continue walking until you've strolled through the door to complete victory, liberation, and the assurance that your life is worth living. Some women have passively lived with abuse for so long that they have accepted it as a part of their daily walk and plight in life, but the devil is a liar! Allow the comforting reminder of John 10:10 to be your guide: *The thief cometh not, but for to steal, and to kill, and to destroy: I am come that they might have life, and that they might have it more abundantly.* Abundance is yours if you're willing to receive!

Horrified, Tamar questioned her brother, "How can you do this thing to me? Do you not respect who I am or who God called me to be?" Anybody who lays his hands on you or abuses you has no sense of who you are in the kingdom of God, because if he understood that you are a treasure in the eyesight of God, then he would treat you as a precious stone. He would cultivate you like a precious rose and value you for the precious diamond that you are. You don't see anyone abusing diamonds and tossing them away. Become secure in who you are, and recognize that you are royalty in the eyes of God—a precious gem meant to be handled only by a professional craftsman who recognizes your worth.

In her final effort to make sense of a senseless situation, Tamar asks, "What am I going to do now that you've done this to me?" Still, Amnon ignored her words, and pursued his passions.

Then, Amnon hated her so much that his hatred toward her surpassed the love he initially had for her. *Then Amnon hated her exceedingly; so that the hatred wherewith he hated her was greater than the love wherewith he had loved her* (2 Sam. 13:15). In all reality, it's not that Amnon hated Tamar, but he hated himself. And because he lacked the maturity to admit that he was the one who was sick, he took his guilt and frustration out on her. So in order to give himself some time out, he had to find a way to release his frustration on somebody who's more vulnerable than himself. It matters not what obstacles a man has had to face in life—problems on the job, being racially profiled on the highway while going home from work, or whatever the case may be—it still does not give him a license or the authority to abuse a woman because he can't contain his short temper and bad attitude. It's because Amnon never truly loved Tamar in the first place that he then began to hate her.

Too often, lust and love are erroneously interwoven, when one does not define the other. The true test of love is when a man is able to recognize a virtuous woman and respect her decision not to engage in premarital sex because he recognizes and respects the God that's in her. Then she can say, "This might really be true love."

THE BLESSING OF A LOCKED DOOR

After having his way with her, Amnon adds insult to injury by calling his servants to put Tamar out. *Put now this woman out from me, and bolt the door after her* (2 Sam. 13:17). He was trying to disgrace her, as if she was trying to come on to him and he didn't want to be bothered. Tamar is a daughter of the king. She's royalty in her own right. She's dressed in the garb of the princess, but after they put her out on the street as if she's worthless, Tamar throws ashes upon her head and rents her robe of divers colors (verse 19). Men who have violated you have disrobed you of your countenance, of your self-esteem and your value to make you feel as if you're not worth anything, that

40

you'll never go anywhere, and that the only way you can survive is with them. Consequently, when they beat you—whether physically or emotionally—they brainwash you into believing that you're worthless. They want to break you down because they're afraid that you'll rise up! Most men who are perpetrators of violence against women are men who disguise their own insecurities with rough and tough exteriors, but beneath are cowardly lions who can not handle strong, intelligent women.

So Amnon commands his servant to lock the door behind her, because he didn't want her coming back in. Women, as difficult and humiliating as it may seem, sometimes you have to thank God for a locked door. Even if Tamar wanted to return to her abuser, she couldn't go back. I know there's someone reading this book who has been locked out of some relationships by God. I know you miss the individual whom God has hindered you from seeing. You've probably been crying over this person because you began to view this individual, potentially, as a permanent mate. However, it is God who has locked the door and forbidden re-entry. So don't weep, but rejoice!

Later, Absalom, Tamar's other brother inquires of her, *Hath Amnon thy brother been with thee? but hold now thy peace, my sister: he is thy brother* (verse 20). In other words, her own family didn't even want her to get help. The family knew what was going on, but never stepped in to intervene. The family knew what kind of pain she'd endured and the scars that she suffered, but they never spoke out. "No," they rationalized, "It will look too bad on the family name. Just hold your peace."

For years women have endured the cycle of violence, while their families have known and turned a blinded eye. The women don't know who to turn to because the family keeps reminding them of all the reasons to keep quiet and endure unnecessary hardness:

"He loves the kids. He has a good job with great benefits. Your father was the same way. Men will be men."

The devil is again a liar! The generational curse in your life has to break. No longer will it continue to permeate your genealogical order, but it must end with you! Even if your family doesn't see that this is killing you, you'd better see it for yourself and realize that you deserve better. You don't want your children involved in this kind of foolishness.

The bible says that Tamar lived in Absalom's house the rest of her life as a desolate creature. In other words, because of the scars of her past and the affliction of her abuse, she never had a healthy relationship. She was never able to have children. She never got married. She remained in her parents' house, because she never got the wholeness and healing that she needed to pick herself up and try all over again. She lacked the life-giving words that she needed from her family to give her godly counsel to rise up out of the ashes and live again.

YOU HAVE A FRIEND

Remember when it says that when Amnon was going through the lust in his body, he had a friend? For every woman who has lived through abuse, for every woman who has lived through violence, just as your perpetrator had a friend, God has given you a friend. And the friend that God has given to you will stick closer to you than a brother. He will protect you, encircle and encamp you. *When my father and my mother forsake me, then the LORD will take me up* (Ps. 27:10). There may have been nights that you cried, and days that you had to call into work sick, but just when you didn't know how you were going to make it, your friend named Jesus showed up to announce, "I'll fight your battles for you!"

If you're dealing with the scars of domestic violence, sexual or other abuse, I want you to know that you never have to live with violence again. You don't have to live your life on the run all the time, constantly running for cover. You don't have to be worried about security. As I write this book, I've asked God to protect you from the top of your head, down to the soles of your feet. Don't allow abusive situations to make you bitter. Rather, allow them to make you better.

Now, for the men who are reading this book... I know some of you are ready to be honest today. This is what you must ask of our Lord to allow him to transform your life and make you whole. Let's agree together in the following prayer:

> *God I need you to deliver me. Deliver me from anger, from my bad temper, and sexual proclivities. God I need you to speak to me because I don't want to continue living like this. I now recognize who I am—that I am anointed and ordained to be a son of You. I know that there is more to me than my animalistic behavior. There is more to me than me than violence and anger. God, I believe that you are a miracle-worker, that you are a healer and that you are a deliverer. I receive my deliverance today...in Jesus' name! Amen.*

We must declare war on the violence that's affecting and afflicting our children, our women and corroding our communities. It's not until we get a defender by the name of Jesus that the victory will be ours!

Chapter Four

INDECENT PROPOSAL

Nelson Mandela, the former president of South Africa, was jailed for 27 years simply because he was a voice for the oppressed. What has not been widely discussed, however, is that Nelson Mandela had several opportunities to get out of jail. On varying occasions, his jailers approached him with the opportunity of negotiating his release, on the grounds that he remain silent regarding the injustices of apartheid. At other times they approached him and offered his freedom on the grounds that he attempt to take no further action, go along with the system, and leave the country. Still, he flatly declined, pointing out that only free men can negotiate, not prisoners.

Nelson Mandela had only been married for about six months before he was incarcerated. He was a father; had a new home, a new wife, and new children, whom he would have liked to have seen, but could not for the sake of his principles. It was a nice proposal to let him out of jail because he did nothing wrong except speak truth to power. But the proposal became indecent when they attempted to compromise his morals, his ethics and his values.

Many of us, on a daily basis, are served proposals. What makes the proposal indecent is when it goes against the will of God. There are some things that God has for you, but it's a matter of how you allocate his purpose for your life that turns it into sin. God has made you and ordained you to be prosperous, but that does not give you a license to deal drugs because you were born "in the hood." That makes it an indecent proposal.

While it is often taboo to speak about the topic of sex and sexuality in the church, sex is not against the will of God. It's just a matter of how you get that need met that takes sex from a desire to a sin. If God gave it to you He wants you to use, but He wants you to use it based on His will and His law. Though your desires are legitimate, you must also initiate legitimate means of satisfying them. You are operating out of flagrant disregard for what God has for you when you take it upon yourself to initiate self gratification with reckless disregard or God's will for your life. So when God gives you what he has for you, you won't fully appreciate the magnitude of His gift because you've already used what he wanted you to save for someone else.

You ask, "How then, do I win the tug of war between my legitimate desires and illegitimate proposals?" Everyday there is something that attempts to make your desires illegitimate when you know in your heart that what you feel is natural. Church can sometimes make you think that what you're feeling is unnatural or illegitimate when oftentimes is not. It doesn't matter how much you feel, how often you fast, or how many conferences you attend in order to be loosed from what you feel, something is still going to reside inside of you to demand comprehension of what you're feeling and how to deal with it.

While writing this book, a young man wanted to share his testimony with me:

"Pastor, I had some problems while working on my job, minding my own business, with my own vision and my own dreams. I wasn't bothering anybody. I was just trying to get my job done so that I could leave for the

46

day. I didn't want to stay on that job a long time because of the awkwardness I'd began to feel around my boss's wife—she kept looking at me in an inappropriately, seductive manner. At first I thought she was just looking at me innocently, but then she began glaring at me, and I knew that we were going to be in trouble. Then, she had the nerve to step to me one day and say, 'Listen, I know I'm married, and I know I shouldn't be doing this, *but* I only need one night with you. You look good and I'm just trying to be down. I just want to know exactly where you stand' [regarding her sexual solicitation."

A similar story is found in the book of Genesis:

And Joseph was a goodly person, and well favoured. [7] *And it came to pass after these things, that his master's wife cast her eyes upon Joseph; and she said, Lie with me.* [8] *But he refused...*(Gen. 39:6-8)

JUST SAY, NO...TO TEMPTATION

Sometimes you have to deal with the fact that the devil tempts you with what you like. He knows exactly how you want him or her to look, how you want this individual to dress, and what you want this person to drive. That's why you should learn to exercise caution when approached by someone in the church who claims, "God told me that you're my spouse." As tempting as he or she may look, rest-assured, that if it was God, He would have also given you the information. Satan knows exactly what you like, which is what makes it such a gratifying temptation.

When I hear people say, "I've been saved and holding myself for 30 years; and I have never seen anything that has tempted me!" it is a clear indication that truth is looming no where within their testimony. When we see something that we like, whether we're saved or not, we often have to fight against our own wills to indulge and give in to the temptation. If you've never been tempted, then you've never had eyes. But as long as you can see, the devil will always dangle something in your face that you will want to touch. When you're tempted by something, it's not always enough for you to just speak and keep walking, but you feel the need to find out who this person actually is. In a lot of churches you find folks who are there specifically to just find a mate, but God says, "Stop looking for a mate and instead look for Me!"

No doubt, God will send you someone who is pleasing to your eyes; yet, He also reminds us, first things first, *But seek ye first the kingdom of God, and his righteousness; and all these things shall be added unto you* (Matthew 6:33). An old blues singer said, "I may not be perfect, but I'm perfect for you!" There is somebody for you whose very presence in the room does something to you. They don't ever have to speak to you, or shake your hand, but just to see this person swells up an array of emotions from within. Still, don't ever make the mistake of thinking that you can not prosper until God brings this person into your life. You are to continue to "occupy" until he or she comes.

Just as Tamar had tried to rationalize with her aggressor, Joseph explained to his master's wife, "I can't sleep with you, because my master has given me everything in the house and I don't have to worry about anything. Look at all that I have without sleeping with you. I have my own house, my own car, I have a closet full of clothes. I have more shoes than I can put on my feet. What makes you think that I have to sleep with you in order for me to be something? I have all of this and I acquired it without sleeping with you."

Some who are reading this book are sleeping with people that they're not married to, and those they don't love, thinking that it is going to assist them in arriving at their destinations. Now, however, it's time to wake up and realize how you've made it thus far. You didn't make it by selling your body and soul, but you got where you are by lifting up the name of Jesus and

48

understanding what God can do, not how far in life your sex partner could take you.

Aren't you sick of folks asking you how you have what you have; how you drive what you drive; how you live where you live? Don't entertain the invitation to needless debates. Simply assure them, "Jesus did it for me!" They can't stand that without a job you still look good, come to church with no money in your bank account, but praise God like you're already a millionaire.

WAIT ON GOD

God is observing what you will do to get ahead. There is no benefit or honor in sleeping with folks, compromising the gifts and the blessings that God has for you. But when you are an anointed child of God, you're not willing to risk 15 minutes of pleasure for eternal life. I hate to say it, but even in church, gold diggers can be found! Within a lot of dating circles amongst those who are supposedly saved, a greater premium is placed on the material over the spiritual. So a job becomes a greater asset than joy; money means more than a miracle in progress, and a car is valued over Christ. The old saying, *I'd Rather Have Jesus than Silver or Gold,*" can not just remain a song, but it must become a mentality.

Put your foot down and declare, "If you want to hear me scream a name, then come to church and hear me as I call on the name of Jesus!" If Jesus sets you free and lifts you, then why do you allow someone else to tie you up and bring you down? With all the many benefits of God's blessings at your fingertips, why would you risk invoking upon yourself a curse?

Joseph explained to Potiphar's wife,

> *Behold, my master wotteth not what is with me in the house, and he hath committed all that he hath to my hand;* [9] *There is none greater in this house than I;*

49

*neither hath he kept back any thing from me but thee,
because thou art his wife: how then can I do this great
wickedness, and sin against God?*

In other words, why would he sleep with his master's wife
and risk losing his many benefits and blessings? If you don't
plan on God blessing you anymore, then carelessly sleep with
whomever you choose. However, if you desire to remain under
His covering, you must refrain from botching the plan of God
over your life by acquiescing to the unharnessed desires of
someone who only cares about self. Believe it or not, God *does*
has a plan for your life.

In the story of Joseph, he goes on to explain to his seducer,
"Furthermore, I can't sleep with you because you're the wife of
someone else." The last thing you need, especially when you're
saved, is someone married inviting further challenges and
 hurdles into your life for you to climb. It is not necessary for you
to be worried all the time; neither should you have to take a
number and stand in line to share the company of your mate with
others. If you can just wait until God answers, He has promised
to give you the desires of your heart, and it won't be another
woman's husband or another man's wife. He has personalized
your blessing, specifically to meet your needs.

Some individuals, however, have become so anxious and
marriage-driven, that they've forgotten how to wait. When you
are so busy planning and plotting to acquire somebody else's
spouse, then waiting on God is no longer an option. Ultimately,
you must come to your senses and decide assuredly, "If I have to
stay by myself, eat by myself, and sleep by myself, it's a small
sacrifice to pay while waiting on God's best. When you're saved,
you have a right to be selfish when it comes to laying aside every
weight in order to attain the specific blessing that God has
created solely to meet your specific need. You no longer have to
be jealous of the blessings that God has bestowed upon others.
Lay aside that cumbersome weight and realize that His Word is
true: *Ask, and it shall be given you; seek, and ye shall find;
knock, and it shall be opened unto you:* (Matthew 7:7). No

50

matter how long you've been waiting, the door is about to swing open on your behalf if you refuse to settle for anything less than God's best!

Joseph's seducer tried him everyday. It's one thing to be tempted by somebody who lives out of town, but when you have to stare in the face of your tempter everyday, it becomes an even greater burden and a daily battle. Genesis 39:10 says, *And it came to pass, as she spake to Joseph day by day, that he hearkened not unto her, to lie by her, or to be with her.* In other words, not only did he refuse to sleep with her, but he also refused to even allow a friendship to develop. Sometimes you must be honest and bold enough to tell some people, "No, we can not be friends!" Joseph refused to even be around his master's wife.

*Learn to be honest with yourself concerning what you're strong enough to handle and what you're too weak to even consider. You can often talk yourself into a maze of deception by lying and making excuses: "It's only a movie. He's only coming over for a short 'friendly' visit. It doesn't mean anything." When deception and the devil are involved, it always means something. Keep in mind how little you stand to gain and all you risk to lose and tell the tempter, "Don't call me, and please don't come around. There is no need for you to check on me. I've found a friend who will stick closer to me than a brother. He will never leave me, nor forsake me."

When Joseph walked away, and refused his boss's wife, she screamed, "Rape!" He lost his job, and it looked like his future was jeopardized. Some readers after considering the message of this text are going to realize that some people have to be cut out of your life. It won't be easy, especially when you're used to having somebody in the bed, and then you will roll over and nobody is there. Initially, when you cut the cord and find that you're without certain people who've become a part of your daily life, it's a difficult place to be. It's at that point, that the devil plays with your self-esteem, plays with your value and with your worth. You start asking yourself, "Am I still desirable?"

The devil will try to talk you into believing that nobody wants you and nobody wants a future with you. Then you'll have to deal with the stigma of what people think when those whom you've removed from your life begin to lie on you. You may find yourself trying to explain family and friends about what actually happened. It is then that the devil taps you on your shoulder and asks, "Was it really worth it?"

Joseph's name and character were dragged through the mud. He had to lose something in order to gain all that God had stored for him. Joseph went to jail for a crime that he didn't commit, but God remembered that he walked away from sex and stood on his godly principles. Just because you turned down some ungodly proposals, God is going to bless you. God is saying, "You're in jail right now, but you're about to be set free. You're about to be delivered out of this ungodly entrapment of temptation that satan has launched against you!"

THREE FACETS OF TEMPTATION

Temptation is like a telemarketer. It encompasses three important facets that get you to buy into what you weren't initially in the market for in the first place:

1. **It always comes at a bad time.** Preying upon your vulnerabilities, temptation comes at a time that you're not thinking clearly and are more prone to make irrational decisions.
2. **Temptation does not easily take no for an answer.** Every time you try to hang up, it calls right back.
3. **It disguises its true identity.** When a telemarketer calls, the source of the call does not always show up on the caller ID and is not always identifiable; so, you don't know from where the call is coming. You might not know where your temptation is being sent from, but you ought to know that it's not from God. God will let you know if

it's from him. Telemarketers always make something sound better on the phone than it is in real life, and so it is with temptation. Some of you have had some telemarketer relationships that sounded good on the phone, but turned out to be bad connections in person.

This is how I've found to get rid of telemarketers and the mess in your life? When they ask you the vital question, "Are you the decision-maker in the home," just say, "No, you will have to speak to my Father."

Proposition is never extended unless the person who's making the proposition thinks that you have some value. People who are trying to tempt you know your value. The devil would not bother you if he did not think that you were a threat to him. The reason that men get upset when women don't respond to their ungodly propositions is because they know the woman's worth. Unfortunately, many times the enemy knows your value before you do. It's not until your value has been compromised that you realize who you are. It's not until you walk out of a bad relationship and *find* yourself that you realize how good you really are!

If you're dealing with temptation, it's because the devil knows who you are and knows what you possess. I would dare say that those who have to fight with temptation the most have the most to offer. But when you start releasing yourself, then your value begins to diminish and you no longer think the same about yourself or what God has for you. The devil is a liar because whom ever the Son has set free is free indeed.

I want to give you a decent proposal—the best offer that you're going to get in your life. I want to give you an opportunity to connect with someone who does not just want you for one night, but respects your worth and wants to love you for the rest of your life. I want to propose a relationship where you'll never be abused; you'll never be underestimated; you'll never be talked down to—a relationship that will continue to build you up until you can look at him and say, "thank you."

It's an offer that you can't refuse—a true and eternal relationship with Jesus Christ.

Chapter Five

SISTERS SUPPORTING SICK BROTHERS

In the book of John, you will find a man by the name of Lazarus who was living with two sisters. Because John was nothing more than a preacher, and not a physician as Luke, all that he could record is that Lazarus was sick and he had support from strong sisters. It doesn't say whether the sickness is physical, emotional, spiritual or psychological. All that the sisters report is that he's sick. In reading this text, there are so many sisters that are supporting sick brothers. We realize that whether the affliction is cancer, or HIV, a bad kidney or blood that is not functioning properly, you know in the intimacy of your own private space, when a brother is sick.

He is sick spiritually, because he will not come to church. He says he's doing his "own thing," but he never praises God. He never reads the Bible for instructions, and he has never had a disciplined prayer life. He's sick spiritually because he wants the whole house to bow down to him, but his family has never seen him bow down to God. He is sick spiritually because he can spend $25 to get his car waxed, $100 to go watch a basketball game, but would become offended when asked to give more than

$5 in the offering plate. He's absolutely sick spiritually. But not only is he sick spiritually, he's sick emotionally.

He's emotionally sick, because he has a problem with the preacher and makes that a problem with his Savior. Even more, he makes it a personal issue so that he can not worship God because of his biasness against a pastor. He's sick emotionally because he does not understand the gift that God has entrusted him with. So rather than affirming and supporting the queen that God has placed at his side; he has become intimidated if she's making more money than he does. Forgetting that all the money is coming into the same house. But because he thinks that his manhood is validated by a paycheck, he's absolutely sick. He's absolutely emotionally sick when he abuses the woman who gave birth to his children and then says, " Oh it was a mistake, I'm sorry, I will never do it again."

He's sick psychologically because he keeps making excuses for why he can't work, but spends all of his money on $140 sneakers that he won't even take the time to lace up to go for a job interview. He's absolutely sick because he keeps complaining about all the so-called wrongful deeds that "the man" is doing to prevent him from prospering, but he has to understand that he will never be "the man" until he knows the Man who died for him—Christ, the One who stood for him, while he was yet sinning. He's absolutely sick to sit in church and remember all the things that God delivered him from: drugs, alcohol, and from the street corner activity, yet decided that it's sissified to praise God. That same man will go to a basketball court or a concert and scream until he loses his voice, cheering for those who didn't make a way for him to live and not die.

From Death to Life

Many brothers who are reading this book are on the brink of death. They're on the brink of losing their sanity, their conscience, their dreams, their goals and their ambitions. The only reason that they're not dead yet, in jail, or somewhere passed out on a street corner, is because a woman had the courage to yank his collar and say, " You are created for more than this. You can be a better husband. You can be a better father. You can be a better leader!" Men, you must realize that there is more to life than wearing a beeper or cell phone on your hip. The important questions to ask are, "Do you know how to talk to the woman in your life, or your children? Do you know how to speak up for issues in your community? Do you know the true and living God?" It is now time for us to begin holding each other accountable. It is my earnest prayer that you refuse to read this book and then resort to life as usual. By the time you reach its conclusion, complete healing will be your portion.

Lazarus was sick unto death and sisters supported him. In the first instance of supporting him, they called his name. They didn't talk about him, scandalize him, or post his idiosyncrasies and shortcomings on the internet. They did not talk about him at choir rehearsal or in the beauty salon. But the sisters surmised, "If we want this brother healed, then we need to call his name to God." The bible records them as saying, "Jesus, come quickly! Your brother Lazarus, who is sick, needs your immediate attention!"

Sisters, in this book, I need you to fill in the name of the man that you need God to change this year. God said, "If you have enough faith to call that man's name, then I'm on my way."

Before you write that man's name, there's another name that you must call out loud right now. The Bible says that they sent a two-way page to Jesus and said, "Lord come quick!" If you need God to save a man who's in your life, first you'd better start calling on the name of Jesus.

This is the year that _____ is going to be a father
This is the year that _____ is going to be a husb*
This is the year _____ is going to be a lea*
Jesus' name. I dare you to take out your pen and writ*
right now!

Do you realize that at the name Jesus every knee must bow and every tongue must confess? Do you know that if you call on the name of Jesus, demons must flee! They called his name and said, "Lord the one you love is sick."

The book of John, shares with us some insightful information about the relationship between the sisters and the brother. He categorizes and defined the relationship of the brother through the sisters. Lazarus was the brother to the sister who had enough sense to worship God, when God showed up. Nowhere in the Bible do we find that Lazarus was a worshipper, but because he was associated and connected to a woman who was a praiser, God knew him through that woman. Because of the praise you gave last year in church, believing God for the man in your life to get saved, delivered and receive a breakthrough, God has a message especially for you. He says, "Don't think that I was ignoring you. I was just waiting to see if you were able to hold on until right now! So because of the praise that you gave me when he broke your heart, the praise you offered when he backslid, and because of the praise you gave me when you didn't know how you were going to raise your family, know that I am going to bless you, because I'm in love with you."

There's a man in your life who's about to be blessed, not because of him, but because of his relationship with you. And if he has good sense, he's going to learn how to take care of you because your blessings are connected to him. I know that I'm reaching a lot of saved sisters who are reading this book. You had a man leave you, and it wasn't until he left that his entire life fell apart. Then he had to come back, lay down his pride and admit, "I don't know what's wrong, but ever sense I left you I can't get anything right." That's because he didn't know that his blessings were connected to a woman.

THE BLESSING OF A WOMAN

Sisters, do you know that there's a blessing in your bosom and when your praises go up, the blessing come down? Sisters reading this book can you ask God to save that man. There's a blessing connected to you. Do you not understand that any man who gets you is blessed, and he can only do better by sticking with because there's a blessing in your hair, in your heart and in your praise.

The bible says that the sisters supported him by speaking up for him. Secondly the sisters supported him by expecting the best for him. The bible says that Jesus hung out an additional two days and then finally showed up. One sister ran out to meet Jesus at the state line and rebuked Him, "Had you been here, our brother would not have died!" I know a lot of sisters have secret prayers and secret hopes for a man whom your family has told you to give up on. You keep reassuring yourself, "If I could ever get that man to church, if I could ever get him under the power of the Holy Ghost, if I could just get him into the house of the Lord just one time, then I just feel like God could turn his situation around." So many people are expecting the worst from him, but he doesn't need somebody tearing him down, reminding him of all of his mistakes and all of his problems.

You don't even realize that when God gave you to him, he made you a prophet. You have to prophesy into his life and speak life to him: "I don't care how bad your day was, tomorrow's going to get better." Tell him, "This week you're going to find a job. This week you're going to find a way to get back into school. This week your situation is going to turn around for the better." Sisters, prophesy to him and tell him, "It has to get better right now!"

The third way that a sister can support a brother is by realizing that there sometimes comes a point when you're dealing with a man who gets so sick that you have no choice but to go ahead and bury him. You just have to decide within self, "Look brother, the help you need, I can't give to you." In the Bible, the sisters buried the brother. They said, This brother is too sick for us." In other words, before some brothers can heal, you must first let them die. You can't have any dealings with them and they can not occupy your space. You must send a resounding message to them, "No, we can not *just be friends*! No you can not call me. No I don't need you to take me to dinner. As far as I'm concerned, you're dead."

Inevitably, the sick brother is going to ask you, "When can I call you? When can I take you out?" Tell him, "You can not call me. You can not come home with me. You can not take me out, until Jesus comes, because right now your body stinks." So, sisters, there are some things that you'd better just walk away from until Jesus comes. When Jesus shows up, He will turn your situation around.

COME FORTH!

The Bible says that Jesus showed up and said, "Show me where you laid him."

To which the sisters replied, "Jesus there's no reason for us to show you his corpse. We can't waste your time. He's just trifling. I don't even want you involved with him. By now, his situation stinks."

Jesus' response was, "Don't tell me about his condition. Just point him out to me, and let me handle him."

Some of you are asking, "Are you telling me Jesus that the only thing I have to do is point to that man who's sick and you'll do the rest? Is that what you're telling me? I don't have to loan him anymore money? I don't have to give him a ride? I don't have to feel guilty about leaving him? You're telling me that all I have to do is point him out and you'll do the rest?" God says, "That's all you have to do."

"Show me where you laid him. Show me where he is without a job. Show me where he is with low self-esteem. Show me where he is with drug and alcohol addiction. Show me where he is with his abusive tendencies. Show me his secret hide-outs and the places that he takes you and your best friend. All you need to do is show me grave in which you've lain him!"

You know that Jesus is talking to some strong women because in this text He tells the women, "Move the stone." There are no soldiers around. It's just Jesus and some sisters. He said, "If you want that brother healed, all I need you to do is move that stone. Move whatever you thought was the last of him, and if you move your last memory of him, then I can bring him back to life. Whatever he did to you in the last dramatic episode, move it out of the way." Now when you move the stone out of the way, then you have to step aside, and when you step aside, then Jesus starts talking and says, "Man come forth!" All you have to do, sister, is move aside and allow God do the work. And brothers, all you have to do is come forth.

The Bible says that when he came forth, he had death clothes on and Jesus commanded the sisters, "Take those clothes off of him. Loose him and let him go!" In other words, brothers, you have to find a sister who can help you take off the stuff that is weighing you down in order for you to get to the next level. Undress him from where he used to be, to where he is going. And when you take off his grave clothes, replace them with the garment of praise.

What can a sister do to support a sick brother?
1) Speak up for him.
2) Expect the best for him.
3) Bury him.
4) Undress him (in scriptural context)

Men, rejoice, because whatever tried to kill you last year has failed. God saved you for a reason and a purpose. All you have to do now is come forth. So praise God; rejoice, and be healed! For every brother reading this book, there is a sister who prayed for you. I don't know if it was your mother, your grandmother, your aunt, your girlfriend, your neighbor, or somebody on your job, but somebody had you in her prayers. Don't think that you made it this far by yourself. There were some women behind you, who have been praying for you to make it to this point, and if it wasn't for their prayers, you would be dead right now, lying in a grave. But somebody had you on her mind. She took the time to pray you out of the pit of self-destruction; so be glad. Think about it and write her name here. Then whisper a special blessing on her behalf.

God bless _____ *for praying that I would come forth, and be the man that God destined me to be. May the favor of the Lord rest upon all the sisters who've prayed for my spiritual and whollistic healing, from this day forth and forevermore! In Jesus' name. Amen.*

Chapter Six

WALKING AWAY FROM WICKED WOMEN

My sister and I had a very intense argument about the movie *Ali* and offered very differing perspectives. While my father and I were cheering about the prowess, about the strength, stamina, and courage of Muhammad Ali, my sister said that she tuned out of the movie because she could not sit comfortably with his treatment of black women. She said, "It's almost as if he changed women like he changed clothes. At any light affliction or offense he saw himself walking out the door."

Now to illuminate this, you will remember that in the scene with his second wife, while they were in South Africa and he was preparing for his big fight, all of the sports and boxing enthusiasts voted against Muhammad Ali. They stated that his competitor was taller, his reach was longer, his weight was bigger, and that there was no way Ali would be able to survive the fight. Muhammad Ali, who believed in himself, didn't care how large the opponent was. He believed he could take the victory.

In a heated moment, even his wife revealed, her doubt in his skill. She said to him, "I don't want you to die in the ring." In that moment, it jarred Muhammad Ali into consciousness—that the woman whom he loved, supported, and who bore his children, did not believe in him. That was almost a death blow, beyond anything a boxer could land—to know that the woman with whom he shared a sacred space, did not have confidence in his gift.

Many men have not been destroyed by a racist or fascist system, have not been killed by corrupt police officers, but their dreams have been destroyed because the women in their lives, did not believe in them. And if they had a woman who, in fact, was able to see beyond their foes, she could serve as a corner man, and while he's against the ropes cheer him into believing that if he would just keep swinging, he could turn the fight around.

Women, I don't know whether you realize it or not, but you have ungloved so many boxers who wanted to make every attempt to fight for their marriage, to fight for their children, and fight for their future. But because you believed that the enemy was bigger than them, that racism was larger than them, that profiling was larger than them, you began feeding them the negative hype of the crowd instead of reminding them to keep swinging. Whenever you were in an argument, you kept reminding them about their past, their criminal records, their mistakes, their limited education, and limitless flaws. They then begin to believe your report of negativity: "If the woman that I'm with doesn't believe in me, how can I have a chance at victory and how can I ever win.

THE QUEEN'S CORRUPTION

You do understand that this is nothing new. For in the First Book of Kings, we find a man who's saved, who is involved with an unsaved woman. She's an unsaved woman, but she comes to church, so the people in church think that she's saved. They don't know what her activity and her behavior are like after church is over. Those in church wonder why he's no longer with her because they only know the side of her that they saw during worship. They didn't see her at work or outside of the confounds of the church façade. Elijah had a dilemma because he was raised and conditioned to always respect his queen. So whatever the queen asked, he gladly obliged because she was his queen. It didn't matter that she wasn't saved. It didn't matter that she didn't invest in him. It didn't matter that they didn't have the same values. She was still his queen. And because she was his queen, he did what he could to support her, until there was a problem. The queen, Jezebel, introduced promiscuity and brought prostitution into the temple. Elijah, who had a relationship with God, said, "I can not participate, because I understand the mandate that God has placed over my life. I understand that you're still a queen, but I can not participate in an illicit sexual affair to satisfy you, when it angers the God I serve."

His queen who used to love him is now upset with him, because he refuses to sleep with her. As long as he stayed involved in a sexual relationship with her, she didn't have any complaints. But as soon as he shut down the sexual relationship, she wanted to destroy his life. That says to me that today you have to be leery of those who can support you as a sexual partner, but can not support you to do what God has commanded. Many relationships have been severed and broken on the pivotal issue of sexuality. It's all right for you to tithe, for you to pray and for you to come to worship together, but as soon as you get so saved that you're going practice celibacy, that is when the problems unfold. She may attempt to dismantle your entire life based upon her rejection. She concludes that if you're not sleeping with her, then you must be either gay or sleeping with someone else. "If you're not sleeping with me, then I'll put up an antenna of suspicion to make other people think that you're unfaithful and that you're wavering in your ways," she decides.

Elijah tries, in vain, to explain, "Queen, I love you, but I can't have sex with you, and I need you to support me." The queen then makes a declaration, "By this time tomorrow I'm going to kill you, and I'm going to kill everything about you, because you did not do what I asked, and nobody has survived my wrath!"

Men, be careful if the woman you're dating salts the characters of her ex's as reprehensibly offensive as if she's never made any mistakes. For the same way that she's scandalizing his name, when your relationship is over, that's the exact same way she's going to talk about you to the next man. That should help you understand that unleashed within the new millennium in so many of our churches is a Jezebel spirit of those who have the pretense of worship, but wear the cloak of promiscuity. So much so that you will find a lot of unsaved men who prefer to have a church woman. Those men understand that in some cases, not in all, church women make themselves the most available to sexual relationships because they come and have cataclysmic orgasms to release the sexual tension that has been channeling and living in their minds. Therefore, some of the women who claim to have the closest relationship with God in church, are the same women who are willing to give all of themselves behind closed doors because they are not willing to make an even level of commitment to God and who He is.

SEXUALITY IN THE SANCTUARY

You have to then check yourself, because the enemy tries to set up an open-air market of promiscuity and prostitution within the church. That is why, as a woman, you should make up in your mind that you are not coming to church to get a date, but you are coming to church to have a relationship with God. The reality is, that as much as you love God, you may not be able handle a relationship right now, because you know your sexual proclivity is in overdrive, and you're trying to get God to put on the brakes. You know your wheel is out of control, so remember to check yourself before your entire life spirals out of control. That's why God had to cut off every level of relationship when you got saved. He knew that the one area the enemy was going

to try to attack you the most was in the area of y[...]
You could walk away from cigarettes, and mixed [...]
Saturday nights you don't feel like popping a [...]
VCR, or watching TBN. No, you desire the physi[...]
someone to fill the void of loneliness and tension that you've no[...]
yet been able to shake.

The man who has to walk away from a wicked woman, runs for his life. He runs for his life because he understands that he can't stay and talk to her. He knows if he stays that he's going to wind up sleeping with her. There are some people with whom you simply can not have diplomatic discussions, because you know it's just going to be a matter of time, even amidst the heat of an argument, that it's going to escalate to something sexual. But Elijah, who is anointed says, "I know what kind of hold this woman has on me; so I must run from her before I'm pulled back into a basic carnal relationship that I know only God can deliver me from."

God has sent me on a divine assignment to tell you that at this point in your walk, you have to tell the person, "Listen, I don't want to go out to eat, and I can't hang out with you. No, I don't need to go to the movies. I'm fine all by myself, because I have to run from the thing that I know can weigh me down."

The problem with Elijah is that he's running and leaves his brother. In the bible some of your translations will say servant. Another translation would say armorbearer. You will understand that the problem with some men who are saved is that they don't feel comfortable talking to other men about sexual issues because society has conditioned us to feel that your sexuality is tied to your masculinity. So even in church, men feel comfortable talking openly and flagrantly about who they're sleeping with because even in church, there is a structure which dictates that if you're a man, then you have to be sleeping with someone, even if you're saved. But the man whom God is trying to elevate to the next level has to walk away from his brothers, because his brothers encourage him to indulge at a time that he knows he has to run away. "Go ahead, you should do it one time, just get her ur back…if that's all it takes…I wish I had your problem."

t's the advice that most men give each other when it comes to ealing with *wicked or promiscuous women.* You have to get to the place where the walk that God has called you to is treaded alone. Most men in church can not help you get to the level that you're trying to reach.

Some women in the sanctuary will try to lure you into their sex traps. Don't trust people just because they're in church, because it doesn't necessarily mean that they're in Christ. You can get pregnant in church. You *can* contract a sexually transmitted disease in church. Make up in your mind that if you're going to catch on fire, it's not going to be due to a few minutes of temporal pleasure that only lead to years of pain. Instead, catch on fire from the powerful touch of the Holy Ghost.

Elijah runs for shelter beneath a sycamore tree and says, "I'm ready to die because I don't know how to handle this battle between my spirituality and sexuality, and because I know that this is the one thing that's plaguing me, I'd rather die than live in temptation. So he sits under the sycamore tree and says, "God, take me now, because this woman says she's going to kill me in 24 hours."

Don't allow your exes to have the last word regarding your destiny. Whatever they speak against you should become your motivation to press harder toward your ultimate goal. If they tell you that you'll never be anything without them, that should be your queue to start the celebration for your upcoming victory! Understand that God is in the bus stop business. If one bus passes you by, then it was not the right one to take you to your proper destination. Keep waiting, because another one is on the way.

BEARING THE SEASON OF SEPARATION

Beneath his tree of seclusion, Elijah says, "God I want to die." God feeds him so that he can run further. Elijah wants to give up, but God feeds him in order to give him the strength to reach the top of the mountain. The Bible says that it's in a span of forty days. When you're walking away from a wicked woman, all you have to do, really, is bear the season, because you're going to experience separation pains. You will discover that the devil will try to destroy you within those first seven days to make you feel like there's no way you are complete without her.

In forty days, however, God takes him from beneath a tree to the top of Mount Horeb. When the relationship initially ends, he's at his lowest point because he's under a tree. But in forty days, when God gets finished with him, he's on the top of the mountain, which is his highest point. God is saying, "Whatever relationship has wounded you, I can perform perfect healing in forty days. I will take you from your lowest point, to your highest pinnacle." When I'm at my lowest point, I look my trouble in the face. But at my highest point, my trouble seems small and insignificant.

If you've been crying, stressed, can't sleep at night, or even eat during the day, God is saying, "In forty days, I'm going to change your situation." By the time you get to the end of your forty days, you're going to praise God like never before. Even if it's day number one and you can't see your healing, praise God because He's going to elevate you as never before and change your season.

The issue is, How do you respond in the interim period? What are you going to do between now and the fortieth day? The bible says that Elijah kept running and the more he ran, the higher he got. The further you get away from your unhealthy relationship, the higher God is going to take you, and the closer you will be to Him. You may still be recovering from a divorce or a breakup, but the Lord wants you to discover the significance of a rearview mirror. In the rearview mirror *objects appear closer than they really are.* Your problem is that you keep looking back to where you came from, and although it looks like your situation is chasing you, that's just the devil trying to trick you. God is putting space between you and your reckless relationship. Some of us are running in church because we absolutely refuse to look back.

Others would be running and shouting the victory with you if only they knew about the nasty relationship you managed to survive, the abuse that you endured, and the negative energy planted in your mind. Today, however, you stand with the courage, in spite of the near fatal blows of your attacker and say, "Thank you Lord!" You are a living miracle.

The bible says that while Elijah was standing on the mountain a great wind came, but God was not in the wind. Later, there was a great earthquake, but God was not in the earthquake. After that came a fire, but God was not in the fire. You're dealing with wind, earthquake and fire. That sounds like a storm to me. Elijah keeps looking in the wind. He keeps inspecting the earthquake. He's checking the fire, but God is in neither of them. All of those entities represent confusion and God is not the author of confusion. So even while He was not *in* the earthquake, the wind, or the fire, know that God was *behind* it. The Bible says that after all that, God showed up in a still, small voice. When you have to abruptly leave an unhealthy relationship, expect some storms, but don't allow a false prophet to tell you that God brought you that storm. Just know that God was behind the storm.

If God was behind the storm, it means that whatever the storm knocked down, God was going to pick up. So, whatever you've lost in your last relationship, you are about to get back. If you lost your joy, your self-esteem, your drive and your dream, it was nothing but a storm. Nevertheless, aren't you glad that the storm is finally passing over? Some of you feel lighter right now, knowing that if you'd never had a problem, you wouldn't know

God was able to solve them. He wasn't in the storm. He was behind it, which means that God is watching it. He comes in a *still small voice* to give a word of comfort. Perhaps you've been in a storm where you were crying all the time and wet every pillow in your house, but around three in the morning God whispered in your ear, "I will never leave you or forsake you."

It was in a *still small voice*, even while you were driving to church with tears running down your face that He said, "I'm a friend that sticks closer than any brother." When you thought about throwing in the towel and thought you were useless and worthless, He said, "In the time of trouble, I shall hide you." Normally, when you hear God's voice, it's not during the sermon. It's not during the praise team's time of praise, it's not during the announcements, but you hear a voice when you are all by yourself. You have to check to make sure that you're not going crazy, because you hear God speaking to you saying, "I'll walk with you and I'll talk with you…"

Elijah goes to God on the mountain and says, "God, I'm anxious for you, but I'm the only one left. I'm the only one not questioning his manhood due to a decision to abstain. I'm the only man who's made up in his mind that it doesn't mean that I'm effeminate just because I've decided to refrain from sexual activity. God had to say to him, "Don't get beside yourself. How do you sound saying you are the only one left and you are talking to me? It doesn't make logical sense. If you're the only one left standing, how in the world do you have me?" In other words, you are not by yourself when you have Him. You insult God when you keep talking about you're lonely and saved because God says, "What do you think I'm here for? I'm here putting you to bed at night. I'm here waking you up in the morning. I'm here making a way out of no way and you're telling me that you're by yourself.

I like the fact that Elijah is willing to leave the queen because he understands that it is more important that he have a relationship with the King. Wake up and realize that you're not in it for the queen, but your goal should be to secure a firm relationship with the King—Jesus Christ. In order for you to survive you can no longer try to please people more than you try to please the Savior. If they get mad at you or decide to break up with you, it doesn't matter because you now realize, "I was living before I met you." Now the only way you can live after them is to develop a true relationship with God.

It's not until Elijah walks away from a wicked woman and that he experiences wholeness. Sisters, please know that the myth that "women are needy" is a lie. Many men are silently suffering in fruitless relationships because they'd rather be with someone who does not encourage them and challenge them than be by themselves.

Chapter Seven

STOP CREEPING

Why do you give others the power to oppress you? You will find that many people are not wrestling with controlled substances, drug abuse, or alcohol addiction. The things that keep them oppressed and stressed are not inanimate objects, but people. The reason that you've given them so much power and influence over your life is because you do not understand the first chapter in the book of Genesis—that God will allow you to be oppressed and abused by people when you do not assume your rightful place of authority.

The Bible shares with us insightfully that God gives human beings power over anything that creeps, a point which He signifies sagaciously in the first two clauses—that the birds of the air who have free reign shall be under your subjection, even though you can't fly. God says that you shall have power over fish, even though you can't breathe under water. God did not say that you'll have power over the things that live under the earth, because God understood, that the devil is something that must be handled by God. Therefore, the things that creep on the ground are the things that you shall have power over.

The devil, after tempting Eve was subjugated to crawl on his belly, although at one point he was able to stand flat-footed as the Music of Minister over the host of heaven. Music is one of the solo tools of the enemy. Be careful of those who play music to set the mood. Because the devil became convoluted within his own mind and began to believe that the praise was directed toward him, God had to knock him off of his feet and make him crawl.

The reason you're crawling may be because you've never lived right and that is why God had to pull the bottom out from under you. He really didn't care what you did in church, but He wanted to know what you did when you got home. He wanted to know why the people in your building don't know that you're saved, and the people on your job don't know that you're anointed. God said, "Listen, if you're going to sneak around, then let me take your legs off of you, because I'm tired of you coming in church one way and perpetrating the fraud when you get around your friends."

The devil was knocked off of his feet and made to crawl. Sometimes it's God who knocks you off of your feet. Sometimes God has to move stuff from you because you think you're standing on your own will, and on your own power. Now you're saved but broke, lonely, depressed, or suffering from sleepless nights because God had to knock the feet off of you to see how you would act when you don't have anything to stand on.

There's something about crawling that puts you in a place where all you can see is the ground. It invokes in you the power to believe and know, I have one thing to stand on and that is God's promise—He promised never to leave me. If you've ever lived in a place where you're at such an all time low that you're eating dirt, it will force you to realize that you were not made to remain in the dirt, but to arise out of those rock-bottom situation and subdue the earth upon which you've been crawling. God did not ordain or anoint you to be in the dirt, so lift up your head and realize who you are.

HANGING OUT WITH CREEPING THINGS

Perhaps you have been down so long that as the blues singers say, *getting up ain't even on your* mind, but God is going to change your direction. The devil meant it for evil, but God meant it for your good. In the Grecian translation, "devil" means *author of confusion.* What the devil did not calculate or understand is that the Lord knows how to destroy his plan of confusion over your life. The way to mess up the devil is to flip the script and confound the confuser.

If you've resorted to eating dirt so long that you've hit an all time low, hold on, because your life is about to change. God wanted to see whether you could survive the rough spots, but He's about to turn your bottomless situations into mountains of victory! Your finances are about to change. Your relationship is about to change. Your job is about to change.

The enemy got confused because when he saw you creeping around, he thought that you were a spineless worm. A worm has a very short lifespan and is just used as bait to catch something else. Perhaps, you too have been used as bait by the enemy to rob your praise, to steal your sanity and to steal your Christianity. He miscalculated who you really were and mistook you for some creeping thing, but upon further inspection, realized that you're a caterpillar, which means you were born a worm, but will die a beautiful butterfly.

God ordained you as a caterpillar. He knew that there would be a moment in time where you'd crawl upon your belly as the scum of the earth, oblivious of your true identity. When God saved you, you were predestined to change, and when God changed your future, He put something inside of you that would forever change your destiny.

The caterpillar is different from any other creeping thing. It has the strange gift of spewing out of its mouth a tangible substance known as a cocoon. A cocoon is spewed out of the mouth of the caterpillar and covers the caterpillar's full body. What happens in the cocoon is the birthing process. It is the process where you're transitioned from a creeping thing to a flying thing! When you're in a cocoon, nobody on the outside can see what's happening on the inside.

COCOON EXPERIENCES

When He places you in a cocoon, God isolates you and puts you in exile so that nobody can alter the process, the plan or the program. So when you feel that you've been left alone, just know that you're about to be transformed into a new creature. You're not by yourself. You're just in the cocoon.

While you're in the cocoon, nobody can see in and you can't see out. Sometimes your future looks so bleak that it doesn't appear to you that your situation is going to change, but that's just the place where God wants you. When it looks like the cocoon of life will never give way to the breaking of day, that's when God has your undivided attention.

Figure out how to read the signs and know when change is about to yield forth her fruit in your existence. You may not know how you're going go get out of your mess or pay your bills, don't know how you're going to go back to school next semester, but as the singer announced, "Don't wait until the battle is over! You can shout right now." While you're in your cocoon, you have to remind yourself, "Sunny days are soon ahead."

In the cocoon, no substances can enter. So how does the caterpillar eat? If he's evolving and growing, how does he eat in order to reach the next level? It dropped into my spirit that sometimes a caterpillar has to eat his own mess to get strength for survival. This is a great example of how your strength is made perfect in weakness. The turbulences that you suffered a few months ago, the pain you felt during the holidays, the set back you endured last summer, God is saying, if you'll just eat dirt a little longer, I'm giving you a brand new menu.

You might not be ready to go to the next level. That is why you're questioning everything with sheer skepticism, while others are saying, "God I'll take it. I'll eat the mess. I'll eat the sorrow. I'll eat the set back, because I trust that you may not come when I want you, but you're always right on time!"

There's no pager or daily planner in the cocoon. So how does the caterpillar know when it's time to come out? He knows when he begins to outgrow his problem! Some of you have outgrown your mess, and the things that would have held you captive last year, are longer an issue for you this year. You have to learn when it's time for you to fight. Don't ever become so comfortable in your cocoon that you're no longer ready to get out. If you're ready to be loosed from everything that has had you bound, begin to rejoice your way out of your cocoon and move from your place of confinement.

Whenever you're lifting up holy hands and praising God, it says to Him, "I'm ready to come out of whatever I'm trapped in." When you're wrapped up, the only way that you can get out of the cocoon is to start moving. Refuse to remain tied up and bound by the enemy's entrapments.

I don't know how tight your cocoon is wrapped around you, but your praise is indicative of how much you want to get out of there. If you don't mind staying depressed, keeping low self-esteem, or continuing to fight with your family, then stay in your cocoon! But for those of you, who feel like breaking out of poverty, breaking out of unemployment, breaking out of low self-esteem, you need to know that the cocoon is squeezing you and it's time to come out.

For those who feel like going to the next level, you must praise God with great expectancy. You're not praising God to do the pastor a favor, or to please your mother or grandmother, but because you've had to fight to survive, fight to win, fight to get out of your mess.

A caterpillar in a cocoon changes its identity. A butterfly is no longer given the surname caterpillar. In other words, when God changes you, you are no longer identified by what you used to be! As a matter of fact, when the change comes, you no longer even look the same. In the cocoon you get a full makeover. You will no longer look the way you used to look or talk the way you used to talk. You're no longer bound by financial instability because God has changed your identity.

The deadliest thing and most unthinkable thing that you can do to a caterpillar when they are in a cocoon is open it for him because the breaking process of the cocoon gives muscles to the wings. In other words, if you open the cocoon for the caterpillar, when it becomes a butterfly, the wings won't have any muscles. So when it attempts to fly, it will not be able to get into the air because the wings were not developed in the gym. The mess that you're in right now, I just calisthenics to strengthen your wings. The reason you can't get any help is because God has to develop your spiritual muscles during the process.

The reason that nobody can help you get out of the cocoon is because God wants to make sure no one else takes the credit for where you're going. The place that God is taking you next month, no one is driving you there but God. Your mother didn't do it for you, and nobody wrote you a letter of recommendation. But Jesus said, "I am the one taking you where you need to be."

Breaking the cocoon is a personal, lonely process that nobody can do for you. Remember, the reason you've developed from a creeping thing to a flying thing is because when you were creeping, people had power over you. But the place where God is about to elevate you, you're going to soar right over them. Everybody who lied on you, everybody who manipulated you, everybody who dragged your name through the mud, God said, "Just hold on. In a few day they're going to have to look up to you." You have been oppressed so long that you didn't even realize you were in bondage. You dress to make others happy, and wear your hair for their approval. You call at the regulated time to check in because you're under somebody else's rulership. *But seek ye first the kingdom of God, and his righteousness; and all these things shall be added unto you* (Matthew 6:33).

Nowhere, does it say that the caterpillar took flying lessons. There was no home video for six weeks of instructional training, but God placed something in the caterpillar and in you that gives you the determination to soar. So that when God releases you into your destiny, you are going to act like you were born to be there. Some may be shocked by the transformation, but just explain, "This is nothing new. I've just been waiting to fly. I've been waiting to live in my prosperity. I've been waiting to live in my season. I've been waiting."

People are not going to get off of you until you're over them. They are not going to respect you, until God puts you in a place of authority, where they have to look up to you for help, assistance and guidance. If you're reading this book and you've been crawling, I want you to put in your mind every person this year who lied on you; every person this year who took you through the dirt; every person this year who caused you to have sleepless nights. Remember the last time that you saw them? All you could see was their footprints because they were stepping all over you. But now I'm going to make you change your location so that all you can see is the tops of their heads, because you are about to soar over them.

While you were crawling, you were eating dirt and were treated like the scum of the earth. Now in order for you to become the butterfly, there is an interim position called the cocoon. You ask, "What do I do between the transformation period of turning from a caterpillar into a beautiful butterfly? How do I keep myself from giving up on God and the gift that He's instilling within me?" I'm glad you asked. Isaiah 40:31 reminds me of a special blessing for those caterpillars who exercised the patience to wait on God for his miraculous transformation: *But they that wait upon the LORD shall renew their strength; they shall mount up with wings as eagles; they shall run, and not be weary; and they shall walk, and not faint.*

My brothers and sisters, with the power vested in me, in the name of the Father, in the name of the Son, in the name of the Holy Ghost, I now pronounce you a butterfly. You no longer have to accept the indecent proposals and you no longer have to crawl. You will no longer be the last, but you shall from this moment forth, be the first for what God has for you. If you claim to be a butterfly, spread your wings and fly!

> **REPEAT OUT LOUD:** *Lord, I'm coming to you, believing your word, that he whom the son sets free is free indeed. God I know that you anointed me to be a butterfly. I know you did not save me to eat dirt. I know you did not pick me to be at the bottom. So right now, I'm believing you to release me from bondage of (insert the person's name) _____. In the name of Jesus, I want to be free of_____ and all the bondage that has accompanied this indecent proposal. From this moment forward I claim it done! In Jesus' name. Amen.*

About the Author

Reverend Jamal-Harrison Bryant is the founder and Pastor of the fastest growing AME Church in the nation—Empowerment Temple in Baltimore, Maryland.

Prior to his pastoral role, Reverend Jamal-Harrison Bryant was the Director of the Youth and College Division of the NAACP where he spearheaded the "Stop the Violence Start the Love Crusade." His efforts have been featured in many media outlets including *Emerge*, *The Source*, and *USA Today*. He has appeared on BET, CNN, C-Span, and Politically Incorrect. According to Ebony Magazine, Rev. Bryant is one of America's Future Leaders.

While his accomplishments are commendable, it is important to note that Jamal Bryant failed the 11th grade. However, he obtained a GED certificate and later became a distinguished graduate of several well-known institutions including Morehouse College in Atlanta, Georgia, where he majored in Political Science and International Studies. After obtaining his undergraduate degree he went on to earn a Masters of Divinity Degree from Duke University in Durham, North Carolina.

685
800 3695 6655
ON #248C
#13651R
13651R
[34530R]